Simple Solutions
for Communication

Simple Solutions
for Communication

Seven Powerful Tips for
Building Relationships
and Connecting

Second Edition

by
Bart Christian

God bless you !

Bart

Simple Solutions for Communication
7 Powerful Tips for Building Relationships and Connecting

Published by Bart Christian
Second Edition

Copyright © 2014 Bart Christian

ISBN: 978-0-9843263-2-7

The purpose of the book is to educate and entertain. The author or publisher does not guarantee that anyone following the techniques, suggestions, tips, ideas, or strategies will become successful. The author and publisher shall have neither liability or responsibility to anyone with respect to any loss or damage caused, or alleged to be caused, directly or indirectly by the information contained in this book.

Printed in the United States of America

What Others are Saying

"I can't tell you what a lifesaver Bart is—he knows what he is talking about and he knows how to keep your interest. When someone knows what they are talking about and believes in the message, people will be sold on the message. Thanks Bart."
—**Karen Johnson, Past President, School Nutrition Association, School Nutrition Director, Yuma Elementary School District, Yuma, AZ**

"This is a must-read book for anyone wanting the "Simple Solution" to everyday communication. Bart has effectively put this in terms anyone can grasp and put in to action right now. This will resonate from the boardroom to the break room. Everyone needs this book.

In this book, Bart has put together a formula that gives you the opportunity to make the leap to the next level of communication with anyone and at any level. He boils things down and makes it simple for anyone to get and implement immediately in their life. By following these simple steps you can begin to have the relationships you were always meant to have.

Life is always throwing us curveballs and distractions. If you want to get ahead quickly and effectively this is a must read. Don't just read it—study it and master these simple tips. A brilliantly simple formula for living an extraordinary life! Read it and most importantly TAKE ACTION on it.

You can spend the rest of your life trying to figure out how to better the relationships in your life, or you can follow the proven habits and principals found in this book. It is your choice, do it the hard way . . . or do it the smart way, which is learning from Bart."
—**James Malinchak. Featured on ABC's Hit TV Show, "Secret Millionaire"**
Co-Author, *Chicken Soup for the College Soul*
Founder, www.BigMoneySpeaker.com

"What do profound, interesting, funny and imaginative all have in common? The answer is the author of this book, my friend, Bart Christian. I have spent my career showing people and organizations how to do better and be better. That's why I like this book … Bart shows without a doubt that most of us take the wrong approach to dealing with difficult people in work and in life. The best thing about this book is that Bart will give you simple solutions to unravel what can be a complex subject and instead make it exceptionally easy for all to understand. This book will help you turn the most difficult, impossible and unreachable people in your life into the most devoted and loyal colleagues and lifetime friends. No matter what your profession or job title you will benefit from the content in this book. If you want to make a difference in your life then Bart's book is one that you want on your bookshelf."
—**Craig Weidel, SNS, MNLP, MHT, CHt., NLP - 'The Child Nutrition Guy' Speaker, Author, Coach, CEO of Speaking Dynamic Concepts, LLC**

"Finally! Something simple and not over complicated. Simple habits that we can all identify and make part of our daily routine. Just follow Bart's instructions and you will grow your connection in relationships at home, work and in life."
—**Jonathan Sprinkles, "Your Connection Coach", TV Personality, Author, National Speaker of the Year**

"This wonderful and Insightful book shows you how to be more persuasive and influential, and get you ideas across faster than ever."
—**Brian Tracy, Top selling author of over 45 books and has addressed more than 4,000,000 people in over 4000 talks and seminars worldwide**

Bart Christian

The Ideal Choice For A Speaker At Your Next Event!

Programs can be tailored to fit your theme of:

Professional Growth, Personal Development, Team Building, Coaching Staff, Leadership, Change, Motivating Staff, etc.

To Check Availability or for More Information:
Call: 1 (888) 838-1550 or (520) 744-1092
Email: bart@bartchristian.com
www.BartChristian.com

Dedication

This book is dedicated to my wife, Melisa. You have stood by me for more than a quarter century and taught me so much about communication. I have never doubted your love and faith in me.

I also want to mention my good friends and mentors Lou Volpe and James Malinchak, who motivated me to put my thoughts down on paper. And to my mother and father who always have believed in me, even when I did not.

Overshadowing all of this are the blessings that almighty God has given to me through good friends, health, and a loving family. All the honor and glory are due Him.

Romans 8:28-30

Acknowledgements

These days it seems that the simple art of saying "Thank you" has been all but lost. That's a real shame because those two words (along with "I am sorry") can be game changers in both relationships and business. So without wasting another word, I want to say *thank you* to a few special people who have meant so much to my business and me.

First of all, to my coach, James Malinchak, thank you for giving me the opportunity to grow on stage and for showing me the way through the forest when all I could see were the blades of grass. I am blessed and proud to call you my friend.

To my long-time friend, Lou Volpe, you inspired me in so many ways over the last twenty years—at first from afar and now as my most trusted advisor and one of my closest and dearest friends. I appreciate you and your lovely wife Judy more than words can express.

To the Child Nutrition Directors across Arizona and New Mexico, many thanks to you for allowing me to craft and refine the entire Simple Solutions series in front of your staff. The feedback helped to make this series a tool that is useful to anyone who deals with others as a part of their vocation, or even in the day-to-day relationships we all enjoy.

If I listed every person in the School Nutrition Associations nationwide who have had a positive impact on my life, my family, and my entire team, you'd be reading the list for a long time to come! So, for all those who have been our helpers and cheerleaders over the last decade, "Thank you." I'm sorry I cannot list each and every one of you. We thank God for bringing you into our lives and building us up when we needed it most.

Table of Contents

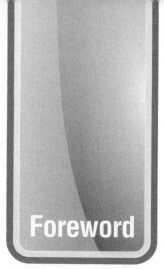

Foreword

Everybody Needs a Coach

THE GREAT DALE CARNEGIE once said that, "People really do not care what you know until they know a little bit about you." So, here is just "a little bit" about me to get things rolling.

In February of 1985, a skinny kid with barely two nickels to rub together married a beautiful young brunette. This beautiful woman became the mother of two wonderful children, as well as a fantastic wife and friend. In case you had any doubt—I was that skinny kid. What I have learned over the last quarter century from my bride and from running several companies is that good communication takes effort, and lots of it. But the payoff is often nothing short of magic in the form of positive, spiritually enriching relationships with everyone around you.

I have not always been a good communicator. Every now and then, even after nearly a decade of study and research on behavioral styles, it is so easy to fall back into the old habits of impatience and selfishness. Sure, those behaviors are considered by many to be *normal*. But that doesn't mean that we should just accept them as *the norm*.

Anyone can attend a seminar about effective communication techniques and maybe even go home and put some of them into practice. The hard part is remembering all the things to do and then actually doing them. We all need a reminder and from time to time a little (or a lot of) coaching.

Our ability to communicate our thoughts, beliefs and desires effectively and persuasively is the key to better, happier, more productive and enriching relationships with others and with ourselves. So, I hope the information to follow will be as transformative for your life as it has been for mine.

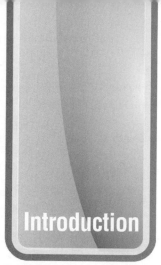

Introduction

Why Did I Write This Anyway?

"How could one innocent little comment I made to my spouse or co-worker have been so misunderstood that it led to this awful, negative situation that has lasted for days, weeks or even years?"

DOES THAT SOUND FAMILIAR? We all have a story about the conversation that started out well but ended badly. It seems the art of communication is a dying skill that few today take the time to consider, much less take the time to practice.

Dale Carnegie once said that, "People will not care what you know until they know that you care." My goal with this book is to share with you the lessons I have learned—many times the HARD way—throughout my life when it comes to communicating with others, and especially with those people you care for the most. If I can save you a misstep or some heartache, then the investment will have been worth it for me and for you.

When considering communication with co-workers, your family, and others, the ultimate goal is to get the most out of the words you use. For this to happen, we must consider three basic things:

1. What are the general challenges with all people?

2. What is your personal communication style?

3. How do you adapt to other people's styles?

It is important for you to understand, first and foremost, that people mostly hear only what they want to hear. To make this more challenging, we all share this great misconception about communication, which is this: *Communication has been achieved simply by verbally sharing instructions or our perspective.* We can easily be misunderstood or unintentionally misleading if we do not make the effort to initially recognize our own personal tendencies and then meet others where they are, both mentally and emotionally.

We all share this great misconception about communication, which is that it has been achieved simply by verbally sharing instructions or our perspective.

To make things worse, we have all the electronic tools that make it so easy to text, email, and jump on Facebook and Twitter. And as a culture, these modern "conveniences" seem to be robbing us of our ability to carry on even simple conversations. Don't believe me? Just venture out into the local mall and talk with a young person or observe them in a public place.

Then there are those "old dogs" that will use the familiar excuse, "This is just the way I am, and I'm too old to change now." But what they are really saying is, "I am too selfish, too lazy, or too insecure to make adjustments for anyone else. The situation is just not that important to me." That may sound a little harsh, but we have all seen it.

We have also seen or heard about that person, who suddenly makes the decision to make a drastic job change, pick up a new daring hobby, or finally sign up for classes at the local community college. The point is that we can change if a situation or person is important to us.

> *If the "why" is big enough, we will figure out*
> *the "how" and then make it happen.*

The inspirational legend Zig Ziglar influenced me in so many ways, but there were two things in particular that have stuck over the years. First, he told me, "Bart, if you help enough other people get what they want from life, then you will be able to have everything you want." My natural question to him was, "So, what do people really want?" Zig said it was simple: "People, in general, have three basic desires—to feel relatively secure, happy, and significant."

The second thing Zig told me changed my life and is actually the reason I wrote this book. He advised me to handle everyone I came into contact with every day as though they have a sign on their back that reads, "Please treat me as if I were important." This is a habit, and once I started treating others with the same respect that I wanted to be treated, the world, in many ways, changed for me.

I make you this promise: If you will open your mind and let go of some old ways of thinking, the concepts and simple tips in this book *can* and *will* energize your interactions with others, recharge your relationships, and may even change your life for the better.

> *"Handle everyone like they are wearing a sign that reads: 'Treat me as if I were important.'"*
>
> **– Zig Ziglar**

Are You Talking to Me?

NO MATTER HOW YOU slice it, people do not like to be criticized. Few people easily accept criticism and *everyone* resists negative criticism. However, if the critique is offered in a calm and constructive manner, there is a much better chance of it being received favorably.

At some point in our lives, we all wear blinders to our own shortcomings. And let's face it—criticism is often the only way we can be made aware of the things we fail to see in ourselves but that are obvious to the rest of the world. We are truly our own worst critics, and that means we usually cannot see ourselves the way other people see us.

When it comes to taking the blinders off yourself or someone else and revealing something that needs to change, there are definite ways to make it a little less painful. First, when offering constructive criticism to others you must be genuinely concerned about the other person. Remember, "No one cares what you know until they know that you care." People need to know you care and recognize their concerns before they will hear yours.

> *People need to know you care and recognize their concerns before they will hear yours.*

Offer critique in a positive manner that sticks to the facts at hand. Talk in terms of performance, improvement, or meeting established goals and standards. Never spotlight personality issues or shortcomings. That is just a quick route to needless conflict. It is better to pause, take a deep breath, and stick to the relevant information, which means you need to leave your emotions on the sidelines as much as possible.

You can only control your own responses and feelings. Remember no matter how nice, calm and positive you may be, there is no way to know how the other person will respond. As a matter of fact, there may be things going on (that have nothing to do with you) that cause someone to become negative or even combative.

As much as possible, DO NOT take things personally. This is the first key to being able to deliver and receive constructive critique.

So, like the legendary Nike ad says, "Just Do It." Be positive, be calm, and stay in control, both when offering criticism and—perhaps even more importantly—when you are on the receiving end of a healthy dose of criticism.

KEY POINTS:

Few people easily accept criticism.

Be calm, fair, concerned,
and stick to the facts.

✐ Take Action

Name three times when you were negatively criticized:

1. _____

_____

2. _____

_____

3. _____

_____

Were the criticisms justified and how did it make you feel in each case?

1. _____

_____

2. _____

_____

3. _____

_____

Recall a situation where you were involved in a misunderstanding. What happened?

_____

_____

_____

_____

_____

_____

_____

What could have been done differently to avoid the misunderstanding?

_____

_____

_____

_____

_____

_____

_____

Recall a situation where someone did something that completely shocked you in response to what you thought was kindness on your part.

_____

_____

_____

_____

_____

_____

How did you react? How did others around you react?

_____

_____

_____

_____

_____

"Do the Right Thing!
It will gratify some people and
astonish the rest."

– Mark Twain

Do The Right Thing Regardless

JUST WHEN I THINK I have people figured out, something slaps me in the face to remind me that I, in fact, do not. No matter how well we think we can accurately predict how others will react, someone will come along who throws it all right out the window. Life is always throwing little (sometimes huge) curve balls our way just to keep us on our toes.

I recently visited a Cracker Barrel restaurant with my family. It was a dreary, cold day with a steady drizzle of rain coming down. As I approached the door, I saw an elderly lady approaching. She was using a cane and looked to be struggling as she made her way to the door. Being a Southern gentleman, I waited to hold the door for her. As she approached, I was expecting to receive at least a smile and maybe a polite "Thank you."

What I got was quite different. She gave me the fiercest scowl, snatched the door out of my hand, and rudely and strongly asserted, "I am capable of opening my own door, thank you very much." And just like that she walked away.

I was faced with a simple choice: I could get angry, make a few reactionary comments (setting a terrible example for my family), and never hold a door for anyone again. Or I could just smile and accept it for what it was—an unpredictable response from a negative person. I chose the latter. And to this day, I will gladly take a chance and hold doors, especially for a lady.

I guess you could say that I did get a "thank you"—it was just not the kind of thanks I was expecting. How could anyone have predicted that? So, does receiving a negative response mean that we change what we do in the future? No, we keep doing what is right. It may not always be "easy" but it is always "right."

KEY POINT:

Human reaction cannot be predicted.

Do the right thing Anyway.

✎ NOTES

_____

_____

_____

_____

_____

_____

_____

_____

_____

_____

_____

_____

_____

_____

_____

_____

_____

_____

_____

_____

"People are unreasonable, illogical, and self-centered.
Love them anyway.

If you do good, people may accuse you of
selfish motives.
Do good anyway.

If you are successful, you may win false friends
and true enemies.
Succeed anyway.

The good you do today may be forgotten tomorrow.
Do good anyway.

Honesty and transparency make you vulnerable.
Be honest and transparent anyway.

What you spend years building may be
destroyed overnight.
Build anyway.

People who really want help may attack you
if you help them.
Help them anyway.

Give the world the best you have and you
may get hurt.

Give the world your best anyway."

– Mother Teresa

Tip 2

Tell People What You Expect

Have you ever had to train a new person on the job?
Was it frustrating?
*Did you find yourself having to explain
things over and over again?*
*Did their comments and questions just make
you want to SCREAM?*

IF YOU ANSWERED "YES" to any of these questions, then you are a member of a select club that just so happens to include everyone you know. We are all frustrated from time to time by people who appear less informed than we are. Maybe it's the guy from out of town who needs directions but has no sense of direction, or maybe it's the lady whose computer isn't working because the power strip is plugged into itself instead of the wall.

Our nature is to expect everyone around us to share the same frame of reference that we do. This is our nature, and yet it could be no farther from reality. We all come from different perspectives or backgrounds, and we all think differently.

The people who have "the knowledge" are often slow to give complete instructions or share all of the details. Maybe they are impatient or fear that sharing too much will somehow diminish their prestige. Whatever the reason, we all want to avoid outcomes that include confusion and poor results that can lead to even more conflict and miscommunication.

The secret is to just slow down when explaining something or giving instructions, and then ask questions along the way to be sure the other person is following you. Expect that you will have to restate and clarify direction every time. For me, this has led to lessened frustration and clearer communication with nearly everyone.

As a manager, I have seen many extremes and experienced a lot of frustration because my staff sometimes just doesn't "get it." What I finally realized is that the problem nearly every time is not them— the problem is with *me*. I need to be more patient and do a better job of clearly communicating job tasks and responsibilities. I also realized that no matter the education level of the listener, I need to be prepared to repeat instructions, either in whole or in part, at least five to seven times before it is mastered. Since these revelations, my expectations have become more realistic and my frustrations have been less frequent.

> *When you really want to be understood or to understand a message from someone else, it requires genuine desire, effort and that nasty four-letter word, W O R K.*

The point here is a simple one. It's easy to be misunderstood—almost too easy! When you really want to be understood or to understand a message from someone else, it requires genuine desire, effort, and that nasty four-letter word, W-O-R-K.

On a more personal note—after nearly thirty years of marriage and raising two children, I have finally learned that my family cannot read my mind (even though I often feel they should be able to at this point). Once I accepted this fact, I became more patient and put more effort into clearly and completely communicating, especially with my wife. And an amazing thing happened as a result; my relationships improved, not just with my family, but also with everyone I knew. Life just got better, and I found myself being a more patient husband, father, and friend.

Remember: The quality of your life is in direct proportion to the quality of your communications with others. *This is true whether you believe it or not.*

KEY POINT:

People who have the knowledge are often less tolerant of those who do not. Be patient with those who don't know what you know.

✐ Take Action

List three times when you either felt someone was impatient when giving you some type of instruction or times when you were not as patient as you should have been with others.

1. _____

_____

2. _____

_____

3. _____

_____

How did the situations make you feel? Were the instructions you gave productive?

_____

_____

_____

_____

_____

What could have been done differently each time to get a more positive result?

_____

_____

_____

_____

_____

✎ NOTES

_____

_____

_____

_____

_____

_____

_____

_____

_____

_____

_____

_____

_____

_____

_____

_____

_____

_____

_____

_____

_____

"You have brains in your head.

You have feet in your shoes.

Yourself you can steer
wherever you choose.

You're on your own,
and you know what you know.

And you are the guy who'll decide

where to go."

– Dr. Seuss

Tip 3

Know Why vs. Know How

SOME PEOPLE HAVE A REALITY that is not based on, well, actual reality. This causes serious communication problems because their perception of the facts is just not accurate. People believe what they believe (no matter what the truth may really be), and their communication often reflects that.

That is why it's your job to help others understand the "why" behind what you are asking them to do. Explaining the "why" is often the only way to change a person's reality. "Know Why" is much more important in the beginning than "Know How."

If you are communicating with someone in a business atmosphere about a policy or procedure change, you must understand that you are disrupting a set of habits. Your first job should be to transform the way others think about what they are doing in order for them to better accept the new procedure or policy.

Always be prepared to explain the "why" behind the need to change any set of habits. A habit is the result of what we think and feel about a particular job or circumstance. Giving direction without any explanation quite often leads to resentment. No one likes to feel bossed around or bullied. Short, direct explanation of *why* a task is necessary may not always make people happy, but it will go a long way toward helping them be more accepting of the new way of doing things.

> *Always be prepared to explain the "why" behind the need to change any set of habits.*

Ultimately, what you want is for a specific result to occur—and then reoccur—until it becomes a habit. The way we think and feel about something affects the actions taken, which leads to the habit that produces the result we want.

I know this is pretty deep, but stick with me. It all revolves around the way we think about a particular task. To get long-term, deep-rooted habits to form, we must address and correct the thought process that precedes actions, and this is achieved by clearly explaining why something is important and viable. Once this is accomplished, feelings will change, which will in turn affect the actions taken. This will ultimately lead to correct actions being taken, which become habits and, ultimately, the desired long-term results.

Yes, it takes a little extra time and effort, but what is more costly— the front end investment of your time and effort to help someone understand why they need to make a change, or a long and protracted battle over unsatisfactory habits and results? The answer is obvious, don't you think? In summary:

Thoughts control *Feelings,*
which create
Actions that form *Habits,*
which yield
the desired *Results.*

Like it or not, this is true—life does not give us what we deserve most of the time. *However, it almost always gives us what we earn.* When dealing with others, it is always best to work to understand their point of view first and then try to bring them to where you would like them to be. This is a vital first step in establishing positive and effective communication.

Lastly, I mentioned that some people's reality is not actual reality, and this is partly due to the fact that many see only through the lens of their own feelings or hear only what they want to hear. They can tune out details solely based on how they think or feel about a situation.

This is where asking questions and being patient become vital skills.

Consider this actual personal ad that was published a local Atlanta, Georgia newspaper:

Black Female Seeks
Male Companionship

Ethnicity unimportant. I'm a very good-looking girl who likes to play. I love long walks in the woods, riding in your pickup truck, hunting, camping and fishing trips, and cozy winter nights lying by the fire. Candlelight dinners will have me eating right out of your hand. When you get home from work, I'll be wearing only what nature gave me. Kiss me and I'm yours. Call [phone number] and ask for Daisy.

After this ad ran in the paper, over 15,000 men found themselves talking to the Atlanta Humane Society about an eight-week-old black Labrador retriever named Daisy. I am sure they were surprised when they discovered the truth!

Things are not always as they seem, especially when dealing with change and its effect on those around you. People will always believe what they believe, whether true or not, until someone takes the time to help them understand why there might be a better way.

KEY POINTS:

All People are irritated when their habits are disrupted.

Taking time to explain why the change is important will go a long way toward developing the habits and results desired.

Remember the "Know How" does not matter if they do not "Know Why."

✐ Take Action

Give an example of a time when you were ordered to do a task you did not understand.

_____

_____

_____

_____

_____

How could that task have been better explained to you? What was the _why_ behind the _how_?

_____

_____

_____

_____

Have you ever done the same to someone else (friend, family member, or co-worker)? What could you have done differently?

_____

_____

_____

_____

_____

Make a list of procedures or tasks you have been asked to perform for which you do not really understand the *why*.

_____

_____

_____

_____

_____

Who can tell you the *why*? Can you commit to finding this out?

_____

_____

_____

_____

_____

Who else can you share this information with and how will it help their understanding?

_____

_____

_____

_____

_____

_____

"The noblest pleasure is the joy of understanding."

– Leonardo da Vinci

Bonus Section

"My Favorite Subject is ME!"

It has been said that everybody's favorite radio station is "WII-FM" or "What's In It For ME?" At the end of the day, if we are honest, we are all most concerned about our selves, our goals, and our issues. This can quickly create an unintentional wall that can effectively block successful communication.

Knowing this is essential to being an effective communicator, and by simply taking the time to first express interest in other's goals and issues, you can open the door to increased understanding and better relationships. The interesting thing is that once you show a sincere interest in others, they will begin to ask you about your favorite subject—YOU.

Many times, what seems like a lack of cooperation may really be a lack of patience and understanding . . . on your part! See if this sounds familiar: You go to a co-worker on a break with some type of concern regarding a change or challenge on the job. Just as you get started with your story, they interrupt you and begin telling you about their issues, their weekend, their kids, their cat, and on and on it goes. When they finally take a breath, you have forgotten where you left off, you are frustrated, and there is no time left to address your issue.

> **People will generally react negatively to a situation or instructions that they do not understand.**

This is so common. We all have done it—and had it done unto us. It is human nature, and it can be managed and used to your advantage. I do not mean that you will use it in a manipulative way. I am talking about using it to get the most out a conversation.

Anytime you are faced with having to present or implement change at home, at work, or anywhere else, here is a good rule of thumb: Give the other party ample time to express their personal stance. It may not affect your decision or the new program one bit. BUT (and it's a big BUT), they will perceive that you cared enough to listen. This is a huge step towards gaining acceptance even though you may not get complete agreement.

People will generally react negatively to a situation or instructions that they do not understand. It may seem like someone is not listening or not cooperating, when in reality, it is neither. It may simply be that you are missing the fact that they are confused or frustrated because they just don't understand or think you do not care enough to listen to their ideas or concerns. -

My background is in the areas of management, sanitation, safety, and worker safety training. For over twenty years, it's been my job to train staff to comply with various safety-related regulations in the food service industry, and you can imagine that I have heard just about every possible reason why a particular change is "just not necessary."

Some of my favorites are, "This is the way we have always done it" and "We have been doing it this way for years and nobody has ever said anything about it." Of course, I cannot leave out, "The local inspector never said anything about that before" or the infamous, "Nobody has ever died from eating here." Okay, maybe no one is actually dead because of your food, but does that mean you should ignore potential hazards and evolving regulations? Obviously the answer is no.

Years ago, I learned an unforgettable lesson from an older lady who worked in a commercial kitchen. She was creating a hazard for herself as well as the rest of the staff and the customers by incorrectly performing a critical procedure. In the midst of trying to help her (at least I thought I was helping her) correct the issue, she looked at me, bristled up, and very sarcastically said, "Sonny, I have been doing this longer than you've been alive."

> *The best communicators are rarely the best talkers; in fact, they are generally the people who make it a habit to ask questions and then take the time to really listen.*

She was probably right. But being a young communication novice, I smiled and said in a sincere manner, "Yes ma'am, but you've been doing it wrong all this time." And BAM, just like that, my effectiveness as a trainer was forever damaged and effective communication with her was toast. And it was all because I did not take a little time to give her the "why" behind what I was teaching. I had not set the correct tone by explaining why it was so important to follow the new safety procedures; consequently my influence with her was lost . . . forever.

My best advice is to be patient and always explain why a change is appropriate or a behavior must be modified. In the long run, it will save time—and maybe a relationship.

Ultimately, everyone wants to do a good job, and no one wants to endanger themselves, co-workers, or customers. Take a little extra time to explain the reasons behind a change, and you will find that while they may not embrace it immediately, the vast majority of people will accept it and put it into practice.

The best communicators are rarely the best talkers; in fact, they are generally the people who make it a habit to ask questions and then take the time to really listen.

> *"Wisdom is the reward you get for a lifetime of listening when you'd have preferred to talk."*

The key is to become someone who asks questions when talking with others. "Where are you from?" or "How long have you lived here?" are great starters. Another great question is, "What caused you to get into this line of work?" or "How did you come to work here?" These types of questions enable people to tell you more about their favorite subject—themselves. Follow these openers with light questions about family or outside interests, and you will have at least broken down the walls a bit and likely made a friend.

If you will commit to this and begin to be interested first in others and their concerns, they will in turn be more open to what is important to you and your interests. By embracing this one thing, you will immediately become a much more effective communicator.

We all know the Golden Rule: "Do unto others as you would have them do unto you."

I want to encourage you to also remember what I call the *Platinum Rule*: "Do unto others as **they** would have you do unto **them**."

This great quote from Doug Larson pretty much says it all, "Wisdom is the reward you get for a lifetime of listening when you'd have preferred to talk."

KEY POINTS:

People are mostly interested in themselves and their problems. Remember, people don't care what you know until they know that you care.

People will generally react negatively to anything they do not understand or immediately accept.

(Do not return the favor!)

✏ Take Action

Recall a time when you were "commanded" to make some type of change without any explanation. How did it make you feel?

_____

_____

_____

_____

_____

_____

How could the situation have been handled differently to get better cooperation?

_____

_____

_____

_____

_____

List an instance where someone could not quit talking about him or herself. How did that make you feel?

_____

_____

_____

_____

_____

What are some of your favorite subjects to talk about?

_____

_____

_____

_____

_____

_____

List three questions you will begin to use when meeting new people or interacting with others to demonstrate that you are interested in and care about them.

1. _____

_____

2. _____

_____

3. _____

_____

"Life has taught me to embrace change,
because every time I thought I was giving
up or losing something good. . . I found
that in reality I was gaining something
better. What I have learned is the enemy
of great is very often good."

– Bart Christian

Tip 4

Change Can Be Great

*No one likes change, and yet we live
in a world that is daily changing.
So, what do you do?*

PEOPLE DON'T LIKE TO have their habits disrupted—that is just the way we are wired. However, if change is inevitable, people will generally be more receptive if the following things are present:

1. They have an opportunity to voice their concerns.

2. They are given an explanation as to why the change is necessary.

3. They are given reasonable time to adapt.

My experience is that once the "why" is well established, patience and repetition will go far to overcome the resistance to change. A little explanation combined with patient demonstration will turn even the most ardent opponents around.

The most critical ingredient is your own commitment to the change. People can sense a leader who is on the fence and will use that fact to stir discontent. My mother gave me a little nugget that has seen me through a lot of change: "Once you make a decision, you have to do all you can to make it a good one." Making it a good one starts with commitment.

> "Once you make a decision, you have to do all you can to make it a good one."

I come from a long line of Ford drivers, and as a result, I drove Ford trucks for many years before I moved to Arizona. A good friend worked at the local Dodge dealership, and when it came time to get a new pickup, I bought a Dodge Ram (sorry to you Ford fans). I got to tell you—I hated that Dodge at first—I mean hated it! Nothing was in the right place. I fumbled with the radio controls; tried to turn the lights on and ended up turning on the windshield wipers; attempted to set the cruise control and turned the blinkers on; and blinded many an oncoming car with inadvertent flashes of my high beams. It was a mess for about a month. But then something happened. I got used to it. I adapted, and I have since bought four more Dodge vehicles. I actually love them now. (Unfortunately, Dodge is not paying me to say that.)

My grandfather gave me a great piece of advice that has stuck with me over the years. He said, "Son, change is a freight train, and you either jump on it or get run over by it, 'cause it ain't stopping for nobody." We can fight inevitable change, or embrace it and make it work to our advantage. Most of the time, change is for the better. And if you don't believe that, just think what life would be like if we still used wood burning stoves, outhouses, candlelight, horse drawn wagons, or fax machines.

Lastly, leadership is the key to effective change, and good leadership is founded on two simple principles: *Commitment and Communication*. Leadership, after all, is simply making a decision and sticking to it.

> *"Change is a freight train, and you either jump on it or get run over by it, 'cause it ain't stopping for nobody."*

The bottom line for those of you leading others through any type of change is this: If the General can't explain why it's worth the fight, he will soon find himself (or herself) all alone in the foxhole.

KEY POINTS:

The majority of people are generally resistant to change.

But most of the time, with a little patience, they will adapt if they must. Your commitment level will determine the speed of their acceptance.

✐ Take Action

List three changes that you initially resisted that ended up making your life or work better.

1. _____

_____

2. _____

_____

3. _____

_____

Why were you resistant?

1. _____

_____

2. _____

_____

3. _____

_____

How did the change benefit you personally or in your job?

1. _____

_____

2. _____

_____

3. _____

_____

✎ NOTES

_____

_____

_____

_____

_____

_____

_____

_____

_____

_____

_____

_____

_____

_____

_____

_____

_____

_____

_____

"You talkin' to me. . .
you talkin' to me?
Well, I'm the only one here!"

– Robert De Nero, Taxi Driver 1976

Be There

IT'S SO EASY TO let our minds wander. Have you ever been in a conversation with someone who was just "not there?" Have you ever mentally checked out of a conversation? Maybe you were talking to a new acquaintance—or even good friend—and suddenly you were thinking, "What am I having for dinner tonight?" or "Where should I go for lunch?" or "I have to do this and that later." Other times we take a mental vacation (the beach and the mountains are my personal favorites).

In short, during conversations we are often thinking about anything other than what is actually being said.

When you are talking to another person with whom you desire good communication, you have to **BE THERE**. This means you must be totally present for that conversation, look that person directly in the eye, and fight the urge to think about other things. This is the only way to build a genuine connection with someone, because if you are not mentally present in a conversation, the other person knows it.

Every time I begin to daydream during a conversation, I hear my grandmother's voice booming in the back of my mind... "Pay attention, BOY!!" She told me time after time to remember that the Good Lord gave me *two ears* and *one mouth,* and to use them proportionately. She continually reminded me that listening and paying attention to what was being said are the keys to understanding.

A little tip for being sure you stay engaged and understand is to ask questions and even repeat back to the other person your perception of what was said. This will do two things immediately: 1) It will make you a better listener and 2) Restating what someone says in your own words helps avoid natural miscommunication and common misunderstanding.

Lastly, let's go ahead and get a big misconception out in the open, and that is the belief that we can pay full attention to more than one thing at a time. We call it multitasking—but in reality, it is simply ignoring one thing while concentrating on another. Your conscious mind can only hold a single thought at a time, and the more complex the thought, the longer it takes to transition from one to the other.

Let me present a simple situation that we have all been in to prove this point: Imagine you are driving in an unfamiliar part of town with the radio playing loudly and with noisy kids screaming in the back seat. You start to wonder if you are lost as you begin to pay attention to the area and street signs. Once you realize you really are lost, what is the first

You need to concentrate, pay attention and BE THERE; otherwise you might just miss it.

thing you do? You immediately turn down the radio and tell the kids to quiet down. Why? Because you need to concentrate, pay attention and BE THERE; otherwise you might just miss it.

You may believe that you are great at multitasking, but if you're not listening with your full attention, or you are not completely present, the other person knows it. Question:

Do you realize it when others are
not paying attention to what you are saying?
Of course you do.

Then why would it be any different in the reverse?

You may think that you're fooling people and they don't have any clue that you are really on the beach in your mind as they are talking. But the truth is, just like that person in the car, if you do not turn down the noise in your mind and pay attention to what is being said, you just might miss it. Treat people like they are the only ones there, and your influence and communication success will soar.

And yes . . . I am talkin' to you.

KEY POINT:

People hear *only what they want to hear—and*
this applies to you, too. So when involved in a
conversation with another person—BE THERE.

✐ Take Action

Recall an instance when you or someone you were talking to was not paying complete attention while involved in a conversation. If someone else did that to you, how did it make you feel?

_____

_____

_____

_____

_____

Was there a misunderstanding that occurred as a result? What was it?

_____

_____

_____

_____

_____

How could the misunderstanding have been avoided?

_____

_____

_____

_____

_____

✎ NOTES

_____

_____

_____

_____

_____

_____

_____

_____

_____

_____

_____

_____

_____

_____

_____

_____

_____

_____

_____

_____

_____

_____

"Peace is not the absence of conflict. It is the ability to handle conflict by peaceful means."

– Ronald Reagan

Tip 6

Overcome Workplace Conflict

COMMUNICATION IN THE WORKPLACE carries the same issues as it does in other communication situations. However, when it comes to work conflicts, there are a few specific things to consider. Like many of you, I often spend more hours with my staff than I do with my family, especially during the week. As a result, many workplaces become much like a family environment, which is why the old adage, "You can choose your friends, but you can't choose your family" applies to your co-workers as well.

The world can be a mighty confusing place, and that confusion is never more evident than during times of conflict. Be it an argument at work or home, a debate on television, or a discussion about a sporting event, many people are just so absorbed in their personal picture of how things ought to be that they do not take the time to see things as they really are. It is human nature to want things our way, and in this overly prideful culture, the disease of self-fulfillment is seemingly terminal—*terminal* in that even though we all see it in others, precious few are willing to see it in themselves.

Over the course of the last decade, it has been my goal to understand and to practice the old Native American proverb that says, "Great Spirit, help me never to judge another until I have walked in his moccasins." This has helped tremendously in seeing the pain of other people and how it manifests itself in their relations with others. I have found that conflict is, more times than not, a result of something that has absolutely nothing to do with the issue at hand. Marital or family problems,

> *The question we are all faced with is: Do we really work to put ourselves in the "moccasins" of others?*

illness, spiritual doubts, and the growing plague of narcissism top the list of things I have found at the root of many of the conflicts I have been called in to mediate. What I learned is that there is a second part to the above proverb that most have never heard that says, "Until you walk a mile in another man's moccasins, you can't imagine the smell."

So the real question we all are faced with is: Do we work to put ourselves in the "moccasins" of others, no matter the smell? Of course, there will be those who will attempt to unfairly hurt or betray you for no real reason other than jealousy (they may be jealous of your success, hair color, happiness, shoe size, or who knows what else). The giant step in understanding is that these are really just "things," and these hurtful people have no more control over you than you allow them to have. Your attitude and emotions can only be lost if you choose to give them away.

Conversely, issues that may seem petty and even immature to you may be of great importance to someone else. So, here comes the part about "walking in his moccasins." The hardest thing to do, and the most personally rewarding, is to take a deep breath and not react to whatever the other person may be saying, however inane or childish it may seem to you. Ask yourself an honest question: "What could possibly be motivating this individual to act this way, and of what real profit to me is an angry reaction?" This is the first step toward understanding others and ultimately getting a larger portion (or maybe even all) of what you want.

Much like at home, most conflict or communication problems in a work environment can be narrowed down to these four specific issues.

I. Control

Many conflicts revolve around someone attempting to keep or to restore control. In twenty plus years as a trainer, I have found that the majority of the time, a conflict in the workplace has to do with someone either trying to keep control or restore perceived control over a task or situation.

I have been in many situations working with people on a new procedure, new policy, or just a new way of doing things in their facility. When a conflict arose, it almost always was because they wanted to continue to do it their way instead of the new way.

When seeking advice on family matters, my mother has told me many times, "You have to learn to pick your battles." This valuable advice applies to nearly every potential conflict, and I have tried (unsuccessfully at times) to make this a point of evaluation before going into a battle that very well could be avoided.

This is when the concept of "Know Why" that we discussed earlier is so critical. People who are informed tend to be much more receptive (maybe not completely, but more so) to a new situation. And giving others input as to how a new program might be implemented and being open about the timetable will go a long way towards reducing conflict.

II. Environment

Any change in environment can affect a person's behavior. If a staff member or co-worker has been moved from one area to another, this can sometimes cause a dramatic change in behavior. When someone who was a standout in one area gets moved to a new department, a new problem may develop and maybe a conflict. Remember, people are irritated when their habits are disrupted, and this may be the root issue. A little patience and good communication may be the solution.

There are also people who seem like they are not good team members because they are in a negative environment where conflict, communication issues, and problems are common. But when such people get moved to another department, they may suddenly go from being thorns in the side of everyone to stellar, standout team members who get along with their team. People adjust to changes in their environment, however positive or negative that environment may be.

III. Lack of Appreciation

It's in our nature to seek accolades and praise for our accomplishments. Sometimes when a conflict arises, you may find that people simply feel unappreciated. Never underestimate the importance of saying thanks, telling others that they are important, and letting them know that the job they do is honored and valued. This is the single most overlooked cause of many conflict and communication issues.

I know people who say, "It's just not in my nature to give compliments. As long as they are getting paid, why should they need encouragement?" That is a lazy copout and just another way of saying it is really all about *me*. EVERYONE needs encouragement at some point—and it is true that some need it more than others.

Here is an interesting statistic: The average seventeen-year-old hears the words, "No you can't" 150,000 times, while he or she hears "Yes you can" only 5,000 times. That is a thirty-to-one ratio, and yet we wonder why a new team member is a little reluctant to take on new responsibility and possible risk. Combine this with living or working in an environment that focuses on faults and weaknesses with little or no reinforcement of strengths, and what you have is a rich breeding ground for self-doubt.

> *The average seventeen-year-old hears the words, "No you can't" 150,000 times but hears "Yes you can" only 5,000 times.*

The truth here is that you will NEVER have a truly effective and cohesive team if you do not practice regular encouragement. You will have "employees," but they will never be "teammates" or reach their potential as a group if they do not hear routinely from their leader that they are doing a good job, at least as much as they are hearing the converse.

IV. Stress

In life we generally deal with two types of stress. First, there is the typical everyday variety that includes being late to a meeting or work, spilling coffee on your lap, hitting the neighbor's mailbox, missing a deadline, or having an argument with a family member or co-worker. It's the kind of things that we all deal with everyday.

Then there is severe stress, things like the death of someone we care about, life-threatening illness, loss of a job, or marital struggles. These are events that can stop us in our tracks and change our lives for the worse if we allow them to.

Stress drives people to extremes, and in some cases, it can literally transform you. Stress can make people act irrationally and take them completely out of their normal character. We have all experienced times when a coworker is cheerful on Friday, but then on Monday, he or she acts in a completely opposite manner.

We don't know what happens to others when they are away from the workplace, and many times I have found that when a co-worker or friend is short with me or rude for no reason, it quite often has absolutely nothing to do with me. Something happened (unrelated to me) that caused the shift. We really don't know what goes on in people's lives. The stress of carrying the burdens of family, finances, or just life can bubble out of even the most positive and upbeat person from time to time. The hard part is being sensitive to the feelings of that person and not taking things personally.

My choice has been to look at stressful events as just a part of life—a test of sorts—that gives me an opportunity to grow and become stronger.

It is impossible to think that your co-workers (or even your family) can understand all the stress you feel. All you can do is be more understanding when you see their mood change for no apparent reason. If an unhappy person is normally cheerful, understand that there are forces at work that you simply cannot see.

Personally, I have become much more sensitive to the mood changes of those around me. I have also learned that while we cannot control the events around us, we *can* control our emotional responses and our view of stress, which will then dictate our response. My choice has been to, as much as possible, look at stressful events as just a part of life—a test of sorts—that gives me an opportunity to grow and become stronger.

I have taken to heart the words from Scripture that tell us, *"Consider it a sheer gift, friends, when tests and challenges come at you from all sides. You know that under pressure, your faith-life (your character) is forced into the open and shows its true colors. So don't try to get out of anything prematurely. Let it do its work so you become mature and well-developed, not deficient in any way."*

KEY POINTS:

Be aware of dramatic behavior shifts in yourself and those with whom you work. Focus on being sympathetic, while at the same time being cautious about the battles you choose during these times. These situations will not last forever but can drive people to extremes from time to time.

Arguments are seldom (if ever) won by agreeing or disagreeing for the sake of short-term peace.

Deal with it NOW.

Stress is a natural part of everyone's life.

Don't fight it so hard that you miss the opportunity to learn and to grow from it.

"Whatever" is NEVER the Right Answer!

Is it okay if I give you a little extra here? I thought so!!

AT SOME POINT IN our lives, most of us have ended an argument with this infamous reply: *"Whatever! You're always right."* Have you ever had that word used by someone else to end a conversation with you? It is frustrating and generally only serves to make the situation worse.

"Whatever" is a term of dismissal and simply puts off an inevitable conflict. In our family, we have made that word taboo unless it is followed by, "Whatever you need, Dad" or "Whatever I can do to help." It has its place, and that place is not at the end of an unresolved argument.

I often hear kids and adults using the "whatever" response and then wonder why others just don't get it. The problem is that there is *nothing to get.* This response usually has only one of two meanings. It either means, "I give up on this conversation" or "I do not care enough about you or this issue to talk anymore."

My standard response when someone uses "whatever" in a conversation is to ask two simple questions very patiently and directly:

1. What is it that you mean by that?

2. I would like to understand how you feel. Would you help me to do that?

The situation almost always calms down, or at least stops escalating, because suddenly I have turned it around and asked for the person's help. Remember, "People don't care what you know until they know that you care."

Take the time to hear an opposing viewpoint and then respond thoughtfully. In nearly every case, this leads to a mutual understanding of each other's position. This is the basis for resolving conflict positively and in a way that can be a win-win for everyone.

Arguments need to be resolved or at least addressed as close to immediately as possible. False accommodation of a "whatever" only postpones a conflict to a later date, and often times, it becomes an even more intense argument when it resurfaces for Round Two.

Remember, everyone wants to be heard. Sometimes people just need to get it all out before they can see your side. Many times, if you allow other people to completely make their point, they may just convince themselves (or maybe you) that there was nothing worth arguing about in the first place.

✐ Take Action

Have you ever reacted negatively to another person because of something created outside of that relationship? What caused the difficulty?

_____

_____

_____

_____

_____

How could you have handled the situation differently?

_____

_____

_____

_____

_____

Recall a situation where someone else reacted negatively to you. What was the root cause? How did you handle it? What could you have done differently?

_____

_____

_____

_____

_____

Can you recall a time when you were dismissed with a "whatever?" How did it make you feel?

_____

_____

_____

_____

_____

How will you avoid using that term in the future? What will you do instead?

_____

_____

_____

_____

_____

*"The supreme art of war is
to subdue the enemy

without fighting."*
– Sun Tzu

Is it Really Worth the Fight?

WE HAVE ALL HAD some job or a task that we had to perform that really seemed, well... kinda stupid. It was mundane, repetitive, no one wanted to do it, or it created conflict in some way. However, management deemed it necessary, and it caused problems for you and the organization if it were not done. Here is a story about such a task:

Keeping daily task logs are a common aspect of life in many facilities where I have worked. In one particular facility, the daily logs included recording cooling temperatures of various pieces of equipment. It was a job that was performed twice daily and took less than ten minutes total (five minutes in the AM and five in the PM). The manager was an excellent delegator and had decided that the responsibility for keeping these logs would rotate through the staff daily. There were five people in the site, and each one kept these logs on his or her assigned day.

This sounds easy enough, right? What problems could arise from a once-a-week, ten-minute task? In an effort to make things as easy as possible, the manager had mounted clipboards with the log sheets beside each piece of equipment and attached blue ballpoint pens to the clipboards so that the task could be performed quickly.

Again, where could there possibly be a problem? What ensued was a battle that had the five co-workers in constant conflict and the manager caught square in the middle over—you will never guess—the ink color used for the reports.

At this particular site, there was a little lady who just loved the color green. As a matter of a fact, she wore green almost every day. She had a green coffee cup sitting on her desk atop a handmade green doily. And in that coffee cup she had a lifetime supply of green ballpoint pens filled with, as I'm sure you can guess, green ink.

When this lady's turn came every week to fill out the prescribed logs, she used her green ink pen, which drove half of her co-workers crazy. The other half didn't care, and the manager just wanted the logs done. But the arguments between the green lover and the green pen haters got heated, and feelings were hurt, all over less than a thimble full of green ink. *How ridiculous is that?*

It's important to know what things you really consider valuable enough to put on the gloves for and protect.

This is what happens when people do not know what is really important and they lose sight of what is worth fighting for. My grandmother always told me, "A person who believes in nothing will fall for anything." And I will add that a person who does not recognize the important things will fight over *everything*, no matter how insignificant. Like green ink.

What is worth fighting over in this life? Many times it seems that we get drawn into a conflict that—if we stopped and thought about what the conflict is really about—is downright trivial. At these moments, it's important to know what things you really consider valuable enough to *put on the gloves* for and protect.

I believe that the #1 source of many conflicts is a lack of attention to the vital role that attitude plays in everything we do. For me, my attitude almost always affects my choices. When I have allowed something I have absolutely no control over like the weather, the economy, or the myriad of negative news stories that pummel our minds everyday to affect me, I tend to make poor choices at work and at home.

The choices you make every day are determined by your attitude and can also be, if you allow, influenced by the attitudes of those around you. Simply put, you "make your own bed" most of the time. You have a choice to be positive or negative, and the world around you will reveal the effects of your choice.

Here is a great quote I heard once that says, "Life seldom gives us what we deserve, but it almost always gives us what we earn." So a question we all have to honestly ask ourselves is. "What am I really EARNING for myself?"

The most important "earning" choice you can make is to protect your most precious possession, the one thing that influences your day more than anything else—and that is your attitude. Many of us do not do enough to fight the daily, sometimes hourly, assaults on our state of mind. That is why the most important part of your day is the first thirty minutes, with the first five minutes being the most critical.

When you open your eyes in the morning, what is your first thought? Are you an, "Oh no. Not another day of work!" kind of person? Or maybe you think, "Thank you for another day. I have a good home and I have my health. I get to go to work. It is going to be a great day and I am blessed." I guarantee you that the person who greets the day with a positive and grateful spirit will be better equipped to handle the challenges that the day brings and be someone that others will enjoy being around.

"Life seldom gives us what we deserve, but it almost always gives us what we earn."

Once you have started your day off positively, guard the next few minutes. Do not go straight to the television or radio to turn on the news. You just planted a seed in your mind that it is going to be a great day, but the media will tell you just the opposite. They will report how bad it is everywhere else, and even though it may be thousands of miles away, you will slowly begin to think, "Hmm. Maybe it's not going to be a great day after all."

In a recent moment of weakness, I was watching a local news program that had brought in a prominent stress counselor as a guest expert. During the interview, the host asked his guest to tell the audience the most important thing they could do every day to protect themselves from being, as he termed it, "stressed out." His guest looked him square in the eyes and said, "You really do *not* want to hear my answer," to which the host replied, "Yes, yes we do. That's actually why you're here."

The counselor smiled, looked into the camera, and said, "Alright, all of you at home, turn the television off now. You must understand that the job of this gentleman is to keep you hanging on through the commercials for the next story, and this is accomplished by telling you something so sensational or horrific that you do not dare to change the channel. By the way, during the commercial break, you will be reminded by many advertisers of just how bad your life is— you don't drive the best car, you are in bad shape, you smell terrible, and so on. You've got to take every step to protect your attitude today. Go outside, listen to music or something positive, or play with your children. Just stop watching the news, and stop now."

The great motivator, Zig Ziglar, said it best, "Positive thinking will let you do everything better than negative thinking will." It is a choice we all make every day. Try it for two weeks, and it will change

> *"Positive thinking will let you do everything better than negative thinking will."*

your outlook. Keep it up for a month, and it will change you and how people see you. Keep doing it, and I guarantee you will see great things start happening in your life and in your relationships.

KEY POINTS:

Choose your battles based on what is really important to you. Determine what your priorities are and then defend them, but avoid petty arguments.

Your attitude is your most precious possession. The first thirty minutes of your day determine the mood of your entire day. The first five minutes are critical. Wake up and pause to be grateful.

Instead of thinking about all the things you do not have, dwell on the things that you do have.

✐ Take Action

What are the three most important things in your life?

1. _____

_____

2. _____

_____

3. _____

_____

What are the most important roles you have in life (e.g. parent, spiritual leader, manager, or spouse)?

_____

_____

_____

_____

What are your personal goals for each of these roles? (Example: A goal as a parent may be to let your children know they are loved every day.)

_____

_____

_____

_____

_____

What are three things that you are grateful for in your life?

1. _____

_____

2. _____

_____

3. _____

_____

Write down the names of three people you love and who love you.

1. _____

_____

2. _____

_____

3. _____

_____

Write a single sentence below that you will start your day with for the next two weeks.

_____

_____

_____

_____

_____

_____

_____

_____

It's All About Choices—and when you boil it down, there are only a few things that are really worth the fight. After I first did the previous exercise, I realized that there were just five things that were truly worth a battle for me:

1.   My Faith

2.   My Family

3.   My Country

4.   My Livelihood

5.   My Home

Anything else just seemed to become, well, silly and trivial. Suddenly, arguing with the person who had forty-three items in the express line at the grocery store just wasn't worth the effort. The same applies to that person who cut me off in traffic or whipped into the parking spot I was waiting for.

Life is too short. Live each day on your terms—not someone else's.

"I've learned that people will

forget what you said,

people will forget what you did,

but people will never forget

how you made them feel."

– Maya Angelou

Bonus Section

The Butterfly Effect??

IF THERE'S ONE PLACE that poses the greatest challenge to my commitment to always do and be my best, it has got to be the airport. But because of my job, I see the inside of a lot of airports as I'm traveling to speak and work with people on how to deal with the circumstances of life. *Airports are just stressful.* There are so many moving parts, that something seems to go awry on almost every trip. And just when I think I have got it all together, along comes that moment when it seems like the good Lord Himself is asking me, "Bart, do you really believe what you preach"?

One such moment came at the airport in Midland, Texas.

I had been on a whirlwind of speaking engagements throughout the Southwest. In one week, I had given talks in Albuquerque, Santa Fe, and Roswell, New Mexico, and then on to Dallas, with a final

> *There comes a time when you have to decide if you really believe what you preach.*

stop in Midland, Texas. Now, I've got to tell you that when I boarded the twin propeller plane that took me from Dallas to Midland, there were only six other folks on the flight with me. It was a rough flight in a tiny plane, so when we finally made it to Midland, our first collective inclination was to fall to our knees and kiss the tarmac.

After we got off the plane, our little group assembled in the baggage claim area and shared our immense relief to be alive as we waited on our luggage. The flight before us collected their bags, and then the flight after ours collected theirs, as did the flight after them. It soon became obvious that there was a problem, and our luggage was apparently in no hurry to arrive.

One particularly irritated fellow passenger stormed over to the Southwest Airlines baggage counter and was soon followed by everyone else (all six of us) on the flight. One by one the people who, just a few minutes ago, were so grateful to be standing on solid ground began to lose their minds over the fact that our bags hadn't, in fact, made the journey with us. The young lady at the counter let us know that they had found our luggage—and it was still sitting on the tarmac at Love Field in Dallas.

This wasn't good news for anyone, including me. To paint the picture for you, I was standing there in a pair of flip-flops, my oldest pair of presentable jeans, and my "airplane shirt" (my wife named it that because I wear it on every flight... and it's not a good looking shirt). As you can imagine, this is not the outfit I should be wearing to speak to over 500 people at 7:30 a.m. the next morning.

I wasn't any happier than the rest of the passengers as I listened to them all chastise this poor woman over something that she *literally* had no control over, and I have to admit my first inclination was to join in

> "Don't let somebody else's mess control what goes on in your head."

on the ranting and raving. But then it happened—I remembered the words that I had shared with several hundred people over the last few days, which was, "CHOOSE to be your best." I also remembered my grandmother's sage wisdom, "Don't let somebody else's mess control what goes on in your head."

So, I stepped up to the counter, looked this beaten down lady in the eyes, and said calmly, "I just have two questions. First, do you know where my bags are?"

She replied, "Yes sir, we do."

Then I asked the key question, "Will I get them today?"

She said without hesitation, "Absolutely, you will have them today."

I said, "Well, then that is all I need to know. And by the way, if this is the worst thing that happens to us today, it is gonna be a great day! I appreciate what you all do here, and God bless you."

What happened next is a true testament to practicing what you preach. The woman stood up, walked around the counter, hugged me like I was her long lost brother, and told me how badly she had needed a little encouragement. She briefly shared that it had been a long week trying to balance work along with caring for a sick child, and my words had meant a lot. She walked back around the counter and gave me a LUV coupon. Now, she had given the other passengers a $50 LUV coupon for future use on another Southwest flight as a compensation for the lost bags. But as she handed me a $250 LUV coupon, she beamed her biggest smile and bid me farewell.

We have all heard that we reap what we sow, meaning we get, in like manner, what we give to others. My grandmother always added her paraphrased words from Scripture to this idea, "You get what you give and generally you get more than you give if you make a habit of giving." That sure was the case in Midland. By the way, I did get my bags, I was presentable the next morning, and boy, did I have a great story to tell.

What we do and say has an effect on us and on everyone around us. It's actually scientific fact. And in case you've never heard of it, there is a theory called the Butterfly Effect that states that when a butterfly flaps its wings anywhere in the world, it can cause a major storm somewhere else in the world.

That might sound crazy to you. Seriously, how can something so slight result in something as big as a serious storm or even a tornado? I have to admit, I understand the ripple effect, but I have a hard time fully grasping the idea that a tiny butterfly can make that kind of impact.

However hard it may be to picture it, the point is this: There is some type of reaction for everything that we do, positive or negative. Like it or not, every action we take will come back to us, and likely in the same manner. As Emerson put it, "The sower may [make the] mistake and sow his peas crookedly. [However] the peas make no mistake, but to come up and show his line."

It is inevitable that we will experience the consequences of our actions. If we choose the right ones, we'll get good consequences; if we do not, then there is a good chance we may suffer for it. Like a tiny raindrop falling into a pool and creating a series of ripples, our choices create a Butterfly Effect, and those results not only affect us, but they also affect those around us.

When I decided to invest time to understand this principal, it became clear that I needed to work harder to recognize when the stress of daily life was becoming too much to bear so I could take a step back and consciously

> *"You get what you give, and generally you get more than you give if you make a habit of giving."*

regroup. I knew that was the only way I would be able to fight the natural urge to lash out at others. It was then that I really started to see the truth behind, "We get what we give." I also began to see that the return I was enjoying was often even greater than what I was giving out to others.

No matter how unique we may be, we all share a few common feelings. We all want to be understood and to be communicated with in a way that is most comfortable for *us*. Because of this, the natural tendency is to want people to adapt to *our* way and do things the way *we* want them done. But the reality is this seldom happens exactly how we would like.

Just imagine the size of the "Butterfly Effect" if you suddenly decided to meet others where *they* desired, to adapt yourself to *them* rather than waiting on others to adapt to you. What if you committed to being more responsive and understanding of others? Suddenly you'd find yourself being more influential on the job and at home and getting your way, all the while helping those around you to understand each other better. *This is the point where the Butterfly Effect really starts to work in your favor.*

In order to make the most of the Butterfly Effect in your life and in the lives of those around you, the first step is to recognize your communication style and how others perceive it. Each of us has a style that dictates how we deal with others. This involves not only how we give out information, but also (and maybe more importantly) how it will be received. Our styles can be measured in two ways:

1. Assertiveness is our effort to influence the actions or opinions of others. We all have a dominant communication style—either high assertive or low assertive. Highly assertive people are fairly easy to spot. They can be demanding, competitive, efficient, aggressive, and prone to take risks. A non-assertive person is someone who is typically characterized as constrained, cooperative, quiet, supportive, and easy going. You may be thinking, "This can't be true! I have a little of both." And you're right—it is common to fall somewhere in between the two extremes. However, we all have a dominant style.

2. Responsiveness is how we react and display our feelings and emotions. It refers to our normal emotional reactions to situations and people. High-responsive people generally share the following traits: they are friendly, personable, warm, optimistic, and emotional. Low responsiveness doesn't mean you are comatose; it merely indicates a deliberate, disciplined, unemotional, organized, and orderly style.

We all lean more strongly in one direction or the other when reacting to an event, but as I mentioned, everyone will likely share tendencies from each side of the spectrum. It is important to understand this because how you see yourself is a critical first step toward accepting how others perceive you.

The following chart lists some characteristics of the different styles. Check the ones that apply to you to get an idea of your particular style. It should be noted that many have a sort of "multiple personality" style depending on where they find themselves. For instance, you may be very assertive at work and yet at home or in a social setting, your style may be much less assertive. So, as you consider these charts, examine yourself in the context of one environment at a time (like how you are at work versus at home).

Common Characteristics of Communication Styles

Communication Style	Characteristics
High Assertive	❑ Has strong opinions ❑ Risk taker ❑ Makes swift decisions ❑ Highly active ❑ Confident ❑ Can be confrontational ❑ Impatient with others ❑ Quick to take action ❑ Likes to talk
Low Assertive	❑ Generally quiet ❑ Has mild opinions ❑ Avoids risks ❑ Shy natured ❑ Reserved ❑ Supportive of others ❑ Easy going ❑ Slow to take action ❑ Listener ❑ Makes pleasing first impressions
High Responsive	❑ Personable ❑ Relaxed and warm ❑ Opinionated ❑ Open-minded ❑ Flexible ❑ Shares personal feelings ❑ Relationship oriented
Low Responsive	❑ Aloof with others ❑ Formal and proper ❑ Guarded ❑ Self-controlled ❑ Disciplined ❑ Task and goal oriented ❑ Hides personal feelings ❑ Thinking oriented

Determine where you have the most checkmarks in both areas, and that will help you to understand your personal style. Again, it is okay (and totally normal) to have overlapping styles, but you will likely have one more dominant influence and emotional style.

For more information on styles and also a more detailed, "do it yourself" personality profile, log on to www.bartchristian.com.

Now that you are beginning to have a better grasp on your own style, let's talk about how to determine the style of others. When considering how you may chose to respond to other people, you must be attentive and note their outward, observable behavior characteristics if you really want to positively influence the outcome. The best way do this is to look for a "tell." Everyone has a "tell" that will reveal his or her specific, dominant style—and if you will take a little time to observe, the signs are easy to see.

> *We all have a "tell" that reveals our specific, dominant style—and if you will take a little time to observe, the signs are easy to see.*

An important note to remember—don't stop with first impressions. Instead, dig just a little deeper and look for more than one "tell." Usually, it's easy to spot two or even three of them when meeting and talking with someone. A good rule of thumb is that the first and second most noticeable "tell" is a reflection of a person's dominant style, while the subsequent ones reveal the less dominant style and can give a pretty good first impression of the person's overall public style.

The following chart lists some immediately observable behaviors and how they relate to the different styles.

Observable Behaviors of Communication Styles

Communication Style	Observable Behavior
High Assertive	Firm handshake
	Steady eye contact during a conversation
	Speaks fast with control
	Communicates thoughts and opinions readily
	Leans forward when speaking and listening
	Fast moving
	Uses hand and body gestures to emphasize points
	Shorter attention span
Low Assertive	Soft handshake
	Slower voice speed
	Lower voice volume
	Few hand and body gestures
	Leans back when speaking and listening
	Communicates hesitantly but thoughtfully
	Asks a lot of questions
High Responsive	Lots of hand and body movement
	Flexible time perspective
	Tells stories and anecdotes
	Embellishes facts to make a story more interesting
	Shares personal feelings about events and news
	Seeks contact (hugs, two-handed handshakes, etc.)
	Immediate non-verbal feedback with facial expressions and body language
	Generally perceived as friendly and warm
Low Responsive	Somewhat expressionless (poker face)
	Disciplined with time
	Logical (pushes for facts and details)
	Avoids contact (not a "hugger")
	Slow to share any personal feelings
	Focuses conversation on tasks at hand
	May appear to be distant
	Generally has a calm disposition

If you want to take your self-analysis to the next level, ask someone who knows you well to identify what characteristics others regularly observe in you. This is valuable because we all feel that we are a certain way, while others often may see us in a completely different light.

As I said before, it is interesting that many of us are different at work than we are in social or home environments. So, if you can handle it, ask a family member *and* a co-worker to identify your common characteristics, and then compare the two lists. The key is to be open-minded and not take offense if their perception of you is different from *your* perception of you. This can be quite eye opening—and the results may surprise you.

Once you have determined what mix you are, then you can begin to adapt to other styles. For instance, I'm a high-assertive, high-responsive person, and if I am having a conversation with a low-assertive

> *Everyone wants to be heard; however, few want to take the time to listen.*

or low-responsive person, I know that I need to take my time and be prepared to answer questions, offer more facts, and remain calm. If I only use my usual energetic, fast-paced, risk-taking style, the chances of having an effective conversation with no miscommunication are much lower.

The same goes for low-assertive people who are looking to communicate with high-responsive people. The low-assertive people need to speed up and get to the point in the discussion. If they take their comfortable, methodical approach, the high-responsive folks will quickly lose interest, which negatively affects the chance of good communication.

Now back to the airport in Midland, Texas. Being a high-responsive, high-assertive person, my first inclination was to jump on the bandwagon and give that little baggage lady a piece of my mind, too. After all, how hard could it be to load six people's luggage?

However, knowing what I know about my natural tendencies and understanding the effect of my actions, I chose not to "pile it on." In the end, not only did I get what I wanted—my bags—I also got a big hug, a $250 LUV coupon, and the knowledge that I have I left some ripples that stayed with that lady for the rest of the day and maybe even spread to others she came into contact with. It was a classic Butterfly Effect situation, and it was a blessing to see it in action.

Sure, this takes a little effort, but it can yield tremendous results at work and at home. Everyone wants to be heard; however few want to take the time to listen. The most effective communicators are the ones who take the time to adapt to the other person's style, ask questions and then listen.

KEY POINTS:

The definition of good communication is based on the response you get. If you are not getting the results you want then you MUST change the way you are communicating.

A **big part** of this change is to first understand your style and then adapt it to the style of others. Meet them on their terms rather than expecting them to meet you on yours.

✐ Take Action

What is your dominant style in each area? Are you higher or lower on each scale?

Assertiveness:

_____

Responsiveness:

_____

Think of someone you communicate with on a regular basis. Using the observable behavior chart, what would you say is this person's style and why?

Assertiveness:

_____

_____

_____

Responsiveness:

_____

_____

_____

How will you adapt your style to this person's style the next time you interact?

_____

_____

_____

_____

✎ NOTES

"Knowledge is simply memorizing facts and information; wisdom comes when you act on it and make it a part of your daily life. See, some people dream about doing a great thing, and others stay awake and get it done."

– Bart Christian

Conclusion

"If it is to be, it's up to..."

I ONCE HEARD A FELLOW say, "Some things are just true, whether we believe them or not." Even though we may try to rationalize away our desires, the bottom line is there are things in this world that are *fact* no matter how much we want to deny them.

Here is one such fact: If you want to be a better communicator, have richer relationships, and get the things you desire out of your communication with others, then it's up to you and only you. *No one else will do it for you.*

As business guru Jim Rohn once said, "You just can't hire someone else to do your push-ups." Nope, it doesn't work that way!

> *"You just can't hire someone else to do your push-ups."*

There are three simple laws that—if observed—will change your circumstances and make you not only an effective communicator, but also a better human being. These are the laws of *Cause and Effect*, *Belief and Expectation*, and *Attraction*. Let's take a brief look at each of these and how they are intertwined in everything we do.

1. The Law of Cause and Effect

This law simply says that for everything that happens, there is a reaction. To paraphrase Aristotle, every action has an effect of some kind, whether we can see it or not and whether we like it or not. Everything we do or say will come back to us in some form or another.

The Apostle Paul said it best, "Whatsoever a person sows, that also shall they reap." We are like a stone that is thrown into a pond—we send out ripples and those ripples will come back to us. Here's an idea: Make the decision today to send out positive ripples and to not return the negative ones. The result may surprise you, just like it surprised me at that airport in Midland.

Few people understand this basic law, and when the stresses of the day become momentarily too much, they lash out and then wonder why everyone else is being so mean. We always get back what we give—and it is generally in a greater proportion. Scripture puts it this way, "...it returns to us pressed down, shaken together and overflowing." This principle applies to all things, whether they are positive or negative. Strive to be a person who takes advantage of this law and not one who becomes its victim.

2. The Law of Belief and Expectation

This one is subtle but powerful, and it starts with a question: *Do you believe what you see, or do you see what you already believe to be true?* Today the old adage, "You can't judge a book by its cover" is truer than ever. Our society has become so diverse, with people expressing themselves in some strange ways (strange to us at least, but not to them!), that it is absolutely critical not to be pre-judgmental of others.

Not too long ago I had the misfortune—or did I—to be involved in a car accident with a young man. It was my fault. It was rainy and dark as I backed my big Dodge

> *Do you believe what you see, or do you see what you already believe to be true?*

four-wheel-drive, diesel truck over his much smaller car. Not a lot of damage was done, but there was enough of an impact that we had to call the police.

As I got out of my truck, the other driver was getting out of his car. When he stood up, I noticed that he was a giant, well over six feet tall and every bit of 250 pounds. In addition to a Mohawk haircut and two big earrings, I saw several menacing tattoos. My mind immediately pre-judged this young man, and I braced myself for the worst. Boy, did I learn a great lesson.

The first words this giant of a man said to me were soft and quiet. He asked, "Are you okay? Is anyone hurt?" To which I replied that everyone was okay and no one was hurt. He apologized for being so close to me in the rain and explained that he was in a hurry to get to work. It turned out that this young man was a youth pastor at a local church and was on his way to his other job, which was as a counselor for troubled inner city boys. This was a genuinely good guy; someone who was first concerned about others and demonstrated that to me immediately.

The lesson that night was clear, and for that reason, I consider that "accident" as no accident at all. It changed my perspective and helped me start to see many people for who they are versus who I may have perceived them to be. Remember that your beliefs and expectations of others have a huge effect on how you interact with them and how they respond to you.

Believe the best of your family, friends, acquaintances and co-workers, and expect they will do their best. They will naturally return the feeling (Law of Cause and Effect). And who knows? They may just surprise you—just like that young man surprised me.

As a side note, I have to tell you that when this young man's mother showed up on the scene (at all of five feet tall and 100 pounds, soaking wet), she was the one I should have been afraid of. Like my mother used to tell me, "Momma Bear is always gonna protect her baby no matter, how old he is." I learned that truth first hand that night.

3. The Law of Attraction

I quote my grandmother a lot, quite frankly, because she just had such a unique and memorable way of viewing the world. She had another great saying that she quoted to me nearly every time I went out with my friends. She would grab me and say, "Remember, if you sleep with dogs, you get fleas." I would smile at my Nanny and assure her I did not intend on getting any fleas, whatever that meant. It was not until a few years later that I really understood what she was trying to tell me. If I wanted to be the

> *"If you sleep with dogs, you get fleas."*

best, I needed to hang out with the best. The habits (the fleas) of our closest friends will rub off on us, and we will naturally attract more of the same, good or bad.

I heard it said once (and found it to be true) that a person is the average of their five closest friends in terms of attitude, family status, and income. That is pretty powerful stuff and fits into the analogy, "Birds of a feather flock together." Who are you flocking with? Are they positive, upbeat people who are advancing personally or professionally? Or are they the opposite?

What do you desire to be? Do those around you support that desire? Years ago, there was a sentence in an article I read (that have never been able to find since) that changed my life. It read: *"If you can't CHANGE the people in your life, change the PEOPLE in your life."*

Life is short—and we only have one shot. Why not surround yourself with like-minded people who share a common vision or purpose?

These three laws are true for everyone. I encourage you to be a good friend, believe in others, and expect them to always be their best. The Law of Cause and Effect says you will get it back, and the Good Book says it will be pressed down, shaken together and overflowing.

> *"If you can't change the people in your life, change the people in your life."*

My last word to you is this: *Be a Good Finder. Be an Encourager. Be a Cheerleader.* Isn't this what we really want from others? And isn't this the harvest we would like to reap? Well, every harvest begins with planting. So start planting the seeds you want—today.

KEY POINTS:

Whatever you really believe becomes reality for you.

You can change your life because you can change the way you think.

You can change the person you are and the circumstances you attract.

"Whatsoever a man sows, that also shall he reap."

-The Apostle Paul

✎ NOTES

Bart Christian is the Ideal Choice For the Speaker at Your Next Event!

Choose from Bart's 5 Key Topics

Simple Solutions for Communication

(Motivational Keynote 45 to 60 minutes, Workshop 90 minutes)

We all need to be reminded that the quality of our lives is a direct result of the quality of the relationships we enjoy with others on the job and at home. This program takes a humorous and energetic look at ourselves and at how we interact with others.

Simple Solutions for Dealing with Difficult People

(Motivational Keynote 45 to 60 minutes, Workshop 90 minutes)

This insightful message is designed to help the audience recognize non-productive behaviors and actions in others as well as in themselves. We will identify individual purpose and distinguish those things that are just not worth the fight. Also, coping strategies are presented that can make the inevitable difficult situation turn out more positively.

Simple Solutions for Personal Wellness

(Motivational Keynote 45 to 60 minutes, Workshop 90 minutes)

Conflict is inevitable at home, on the job and in our daily lives. How we handle conflict when it comes can determine our quality of life and relationships. This program will explore not only our direct involvement in conflict but also how we can mediate conflicts that arise around us. The audience will learn skills for dealing with personal conflict and mediating conflicts between other co-workers.

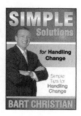

Simple Solutions for Handling Change

(Motivational Keynote 45 to 60 minutes, Workshop 90 minutes)

The most valuable resource any manager has is their staff. Coaching employees involves not only helping the weakest performers to improve it also includes challenging senior staff to strengthen and expand existing skills. This workshop focuses on skills for building trust, listening, providing feedback and understanding as well as developing coaching plans for staff.

Simple Solutions for Leadership

(Motivational Keynote 45 to 60 minutes, Workshop 90 minutes)

Effective leadership is a skill that organizations must have to meet the demands of today. This program makes clear the difference between management and leadership. Attendees will learn to recognize and apply leadership practices along with examining different styles. Also how issues such as empowerment, delegation, and motivation are tied directly to leadership.

INVEST IN THESE OTHER "SIMPLE SOLUTION" RESOURCES!

Simple Solutions for Communication
15 Simple Tips to Communicating Success
$14.95

Simple Solutions for Dealing with Difficult People
5 Habits that Will Transform Your Relationships
$14.95

Simple Solutions for Leadership
Simple Tips for Leadership
$14.95

Simple Solutions for Personal Wellness
Simple Tips for Personal Wellness
$14.95

Simple Solutions for Handling Change
Simple Tips for Handling Change
$14.95

✎ NOTES